THAT'S MINE!

I want it

THAT'S MINE!

I want it

DIEGO MARIN CHARRIS.,MD

I DEDICATE THIS BOOK:
Being universal I believe myself
To my mom, Electa
To my brother Gonzalo
To my brother, Felipe
Wonderful beings
Thank you

We are subject to universal laws and lower-ranking human laws, and we believe that the latter govern our existence, tremendous error of thought, when we thus consider existence.

The desire to manifest, to materialize the desires, is related to one of these laws to attract to our existence that which we long for.

Usually the longing has always been granted, but by moving away from our being, not having the adequate level of emotional vibration, we move away from that materialization.

In this process, we maintain permanent communication with the universe, which has created an accurate map of our vibratory reality.

The alignment between that vibratory reality and our being confuses the way to achieve what is desired, health, money, work, relationships.

Therefore, desire and want allow to manifest more

easily, and at that moment what is desired is created and deposited, waiting for us to learn it materially.

So if we want something, that something must be the dominant vibration, for example if I want money, but I concentrate on not having it, that will be the dominant vibration, and it will not come, because the universe grants us that desire, always you get what you think about.

The awareness of being creators allows us to move where we want, always eliminating resistance, that is, that emotional state where I am and the one I really want, establishing a level of vibration that brings us closer to what we want and have created.

In this horizon, this story unfolds for its illustration, attracting an experience that can enrich its existence now.

Aimlessly I went out for a walk one Saturday through

the streets of my city, and without much contemplation I observed the pale faces of men and women, whose lost gaze on the horizon told me nothing, in total absence of smiles.

In this spontaneous process I noticed that many of the cars were high-end and latest model, their drivers did not reflect the joy of the experience that material life was offering them, I supposed, perhaps because they had acquired the good, it was no longer attractive to your senses.

Moving forward, I entered a medium-sized supermarket, in search of curiosities.

In the parking lot, a couple in their fifties descended from a BMW X6 M50i 2020 car, pearl blue, with long faces, disgusted, physically battered, they did not speak, they entered the premises, I did the same.

I started my shopping, but I kept watching the couple.

They each took a shopping cart and they moved along the entire market, buying a bit of everything without talking or uttering a single word, until they occupied the two carts completely with all possible items.

I dedicate myself to carefully selecting two or three products of my interest, at the best price on offer.

Arranged in line to pay, they canceled a large sum of money with a plastic card, at that time there was no young clerk willing to help them with the packages, they showed their discomfort but said nothing, they left with their two shopping cars and bags, they opened the trunk and proceeded to put away the items.

I appreciated them because I came out first.

Out of nowhere, my being made me express myself in an incredible way.

From a short distance to his vehicle I said out loud, That's mine!

The intrigued couple turned and looked at me strangely.

The male asked, excuse me, what did he say.

And reiterate, that's mine!

What did the lord say?

And I clarified, that latest model vehicle where they downloaded their packages.

At that moment despite the unusual statement, the couple smiled.

The woman addressed me, and said, you are crazy! This car belongs to my husband.

I replied, I don't think so.

The husband, without bothering, asked me the reason for my affirmation.

And I replied,

Dear gentleman, by chance, I have seen you since you arrived at the supermarket, even during shopping by casuality, notice that you look like a couple of robots, you are not living in the present, absorbed in your thoughts, distanced from each other, in total abandonment of the moment.

I cannot find the reason for the use of such a powerful and beautiful piece of automotive, for the nature of its existence.

On the contrary, I claim, that space of life, with my presence, I am dreaming right now of a beautiful trip to the beach with my partner, my son and my dogs, stopping at each place, climbing on the roof to appreciate the panorama, breathing Deeply, feeling the breeze run through my window, I vibrate with the sweat of the heat of the road, I am moved by the smile of my traveling companions, the barking of my dog, and I visualize all this when I observe this wonderful car, it is even the color that fascinates me.

And I'm not even asking you for the items you bought too that would be mine.

The woman totally surprised, out of her being

with my phrases, offended me again, she said cheekily, Go away.

On the contrary, the thoughtful husband listened to me more carefully.

He asked me: What did you just tell me, did you feel it now, or is it your way of thinking and acting always?

Spectacular concern, I felt it now, and my being expressed it.

And does your being always speak to you that way?

Yes, it is a permanent dialogue, in two ways.

What happens if you don't get what you want?

That is something that will not happen, affirm.

Who expressed himself was me, and his information is very valuable.

How do you know?

The information comes from his being, he read it from his inside at all times.

He discovered that you no longer wanted that car, nor

the life experience that was attracting you.

The man smiled.

The wife looked at him doubtfully. And I ask him, is it true what this madman says?

The man nodded with his face and head.

She asked him to clarify, why didn't you tell me?

Not to argue anymore, I'm sick of it all.

And then, are you going to give this car to this man, are you going to give it to him?

I'm thinking about it.

You don't seem very sure, she said to her husband.

The man asked me, what would you do in this case?

I have no doubts, I answered, my heart is the source, integrated with my being and the creative universe, without questioning I would give it to him.

That's mine! I repeated.

Are you sure?

You are not concerned that it affects my life and financial interests.

Not at all.

And you are not concerned? It is a very expensive car, it generates many expenses.

That is not relevant either, at this moment life expands like this, the decision is confirmed.

Totally broken the wife, before the dialogue, I

choose to get out of the vehicle and go, not without first expressing: You are also crazy, if you give that car away, I will not speak to you again, I will even separate, well, that would demonstrate You do not love me anymore.

His wife's attitude made him nervous; I did not reply anything at the time, but when he saw her waiting on the street, I shouted: What I decide is because I love you.

He turned his gaze towards me and then seriously said to me, Will you not be a thug, who uses psychological tricks to manipulate the unwary?

I did not answer him at all, I am a qualified professional, I do not have economic dilemmas, I will gladly identify myself to you for your safety.

Okay

What other reasons does your being give for this vehicle to give you?

There are several apart from this experience.

Your being is asking for help to live in consciousness and enjoy existence, but it does not find an echo or space to make a presence.

He tells me that if he persists in his current state of life, he may lose his partner and stability.

He considers it an opportunity to change and dedicate himself to living at last.

Your vibrations rise every time he considers the option to change.

Without you having noticed this experience has transformed you, your face is serene, your attitude has changed, you are more erect, more rosy, your skin shines, your face has relaxed and you have even smiled.

Your wife finally expressed herself with encouragement, and I offered outings to her life.

The same thing happens to me, I am flowing in this moment I am certain to dominate the world.

So I insist, that's mine!

And what happens if I regret it.

Well, you will have stopped owning a car, since I never regret anything.

And if my wife bothers me to the point of forcing me to dissolve the business.

That duality is part of your life, it is the opportunity to

get this situation out of your marriage forever, reaching a great agreement between beings.

In that space I doubt very much that your lady will regret it.

Okay

I am a businessman, who offers me in exchange for the vehicle. Well, I would feel affected if I do not perceive something in the exchange.

I replied, first of all that's mine.

I wouldn't have to offer you anything.

But, in respect of my being, I consider it appropriate to offer him the money that I have in my wallet at the moment, it is two hundred dollars, I offer that for the inconvenience.

You are a brazen claim. Since this morning I have been very uneasy. Surely this moment was already known to me.

I would like to make this decision together with my

wife, it has been a long time since each one does their own thing without consulting the other.

Suddenly a car similar to that of the exchange appeared on the scene, the latest model, white in color, from which my counterpart's wife descended.

She immediately asked her partner if she had made a decision.

He said no.

Well, I have come to support you.

Somehow this little crazy is a bit right, some time ago I did not hear my being.

What is the business about?

He offered me $ 200, and I'm thinking about it.

They both smiled at the proposal.

She asked me: In my role as wife, what should I do according to your being?

The answer is very simple, you are tired of living a marriage experience alone, you do not share interests with your husband, you have economic freedom and business represents more than your own existence, you want to resume love, communication, dating.

This is the best opportunity to alternate life with new options, this is the first, for you it is a risk, but in reality it is a reality of personal growth and development from the present.

Incredible response.

Tell us about your life.

I love life, my partner and son too, we have been together for ten years, we have traveled together and separated throughout the country, we are happy with everything and everyone, we live to serve.

We work three days a week as freelancers, I am a doctor, my wife is a psychologist, my virtual school child.

We have a couple of dogs picked up from a passing home.

Our goods have already been donated, we only have the right of usufruct until we each go to another dimension, the little one was the one that guided our decision.

We do not watch television.

By agreement we choose a movie in the month of humor and comedy, usually and go to the cinema.

Two or three times a week we go out to dinner.

At social events we like to go together.

We meditate, to be moderately prepared for the sudden events of life.

We have good relationships with our families, respecting their space.

We are fascinated by sex, we have come a long way in their mutual discovery

My son is passionate about nature, we believe he will be a forest engineer.

For us existence is now, they are going to love this car, we have a jeep, as soon as it arrives with this great car, we sell it.

What a strange life and way of thinking, the vehicle owners affirmed in unison.

So, she explained her family experience, we are very traditional, we got married when we left university, we are civil engineers, we have a construction company, we had two children, we have worked judiciously these 25 years, our company is recognized in the sector, we have a high economic well-being, our own house, farm, pent-house on the coast and an apartment in Miami, we travel once a year abroad, our children study in universities in the United States, the largest economy, and marketing the least .

During the week we do not have time to rest, we make many decisions, and we have many projects in development, and responsibilities.

Each one manages their own real estate developments.

Two months ago we bought the trucks, every year we change the model.

Little do we see our families, we go to mass on Sundays.

We have insurance for everything, that's why we do not worry.

We are a little concerned about old age, and ending this journey alone.

Ok, everyone lives their existence in the best possible way.

However, I observe you do not look happy, content, that was what most caught my attention when I met you.

You are resisting life, wonderful experiences, going only to effort, to action, to hard work, and that leads you to spend a lot of energy, uncomfortable thoughts that are aligning with the life system, but not with life, contrary to the laws of the universe, their focus is inadequate and that is why they are not flowing, nor resonating adequately, losing that power.

Observe in this exercise of life, your wife, already vibrating high, when coming again to support you, directed by the universal power of her being, to insist on losing this moment, is to abandon life, ceasing to be the creators of your own life

.

We agree we know each other a little better, go ahead with the business.

This will be a better day, the best day of your lives, watch how your stocks will be different, vibrate higher and stop going against the current.

This experience is a way of acting using aligned energy so that what is desired is created in a more brilliant and intense way, and you will feel full happiness, and the way will be cleared, pure fulfillment.

Doubt is extinguished when leading life is facilitated, the smile surprises us, the feeling of working hard is abandoned, even in the nucleus of the family, relaxation appears, different when leaving the traditional system of life, we move away from the effort, and I'm sure your inspirations will be greater after this moment, and perfect evidence.

It is in your hands to achieve this, it will expand to incredible levels and desired by your commitment to life and energy.

It is a marvel, I have lived it, and that is why I highly recommend it. Simple decisions like these are an avalanche of existence and energy that do not unbalance, on the contrary, they amount to light, to the illumination that we all possess from an original source.

Wow, beautiful words.

Do you have beliefs that oppose this beautiful transaction?

Yes of course.

Now that you are considering the option, what feeling are you having? pleasant, nice, liberating, expansive, or on the contrary, of negation, opposition, and contradiction.

I say this because it is necessary to make a change and return to the belief of source, the natural, of self-respect, of the wonder arriving, and this is achieved by imagining, through a thought of high vibration that feels good, and It attracts, it chooses, to raise the level, causing it to obstruct all kinds of negative energy that prevents you from always feeling good.

By achieving this experience you can control the reality around you, and you can choose to perceive everything without exception.

In this way, what you believe under your old reality, which you will lose by giving me your vehicle, will be updated by a new, natural, spectacular belief that will attract to your lives all the abundance, affection, love, and affection that you desire. , in pure perception.

We all have creative control so that the universe grants us what we want, what we want.

This law applies to me, that's mine! it is unequivocal

proof of the power of that desire for attraction over the universal.

You are being benefited by my natural source, by my modified belief, by my creative reality, by the universe that is sowing my life with what I want, and in turn with what you want.

You've convinced us, the car is yours.

I am in mode reception.

Thank you, the promised

$ 200.

Ok, we take care of the paperwork.

Perfect.

Take the keys and the papers from the vehicle.

See you in a month.

I don't see the need.

Please.

Ok, we will meet, not by the car, but so that I can appreciate your happiness.

Thanks again.

I walked away, they looked calm.

After the month:

Hi.

How did it go?

I see they bought another vehicle.

If it is true, we chose it together, and we go where we like it.

How are you?

Very good.

And the blue car?

I dont know.

Another guy has it, his vibration was higher and he

claimed it was his, and I gave it to him.

And from their stocks, how are they going?

We have been crazy for a month, we have not returned for the company, we do not know what has happened, but we are happy.

Yes, I see their spontaneous smiles, attitude, and the change in their faces is evident.

I'm happy for you.

Bye

Life offers contrasts that make up the experience of existing, always pleasant since our being is aligned with this place, the reduction of this gap, plus a high level of vibration, lead us to what we want, when we know with absolute certainty who we are.

Reading this text allows you to get closer to this place of unity.

The universe has proved to you here that you are doing well.

THAT'S THE LAW

www.ingramcontent.com/pod-product-compliance
Lightning Source LLC
Chambersburg PA
CBHW051401150726
48000CB00003B/1289